Unfavoured Hands

Unfavoured Hands

A Story of Faith, Courage, and Determination.

Nikeisha Henlon-Sterling

Unfavoured Hands: A Story of Faith, Courage, and Determination.

Printed in the United States of America.

Unless otherwise stated, all Scripture quotations are from the King James Version (KJV).

Interior Layout & Cover design by Murray Publishing & Professional Services

ISBN: 978-976-655-134-6

The author can be contacted at:
Email: edugenzconsultancyservices@gmail.com
Instagram: @edugenz.consultancyservice

DEDICATION

I dedicate this book to my husband, Alfred, and daughters, Onielia, Elizabeth, and Joelle, for their unwavering love, endless support, and the countless sacrifices they made this journey possible. May this book inspire you to chase your dreams and empower you with the courage to turn them into reality.

I also dedicate this book to my mother, who affirmed what the Spirit of God had laid on my heart: laying the foundation for the woman I am becoming.

And finally, to every reader who, in turning these pages, finds strength amidst adversity.

With gratitude and boundless appreciation,

Nikeisha Henlon-Sterling

TABLE OF CONTENTS

PREFACE

As I embark on the pages of this narrative, I penned a few words as a preface to the chapters that unfold my life's story. The book *"Unfavoured Hands"* was inspired by God through the desire He placed on my heart to tell my life's story. Join me as I take you on an extraordinary journey through the pages of *"Unfavoured Hands,"* a memoir that transcends the boundaries of personal triumph. In this candid exploration of life's peaks and valleys, I invite you into my world's raw and intimate corners, where struggles transform into stepping stones and determination becomes an art form.

From the labyrinth of adversity to the summits of triumph, "*Unfavoured Hands*" weaves a tapestry of strength, vulnerability, and unyielding determination. Come, navigate the tumultuous waters of my experiences whilst discovering the universal truths that bind us all. This memoir is not just a narrative; it's an anthem of courage and faith and an ode to the indomitable human spirit.

In the crucible of life's challenges, I will share the moments that defined me, celebrating great and small victories. As you turn the pages, you'll find inspiration in the authenticity of the journey and a profound reminder that no matter the obstacles, greatness is still within reach.

"Unfavoured Hands" is a testament to the power of God's words and the power they have to change the lives of those who seek solace in them. I sincerely intend that anyone ready to embrace their journey with unwavering courage will find encouragement and discover renewed strength for the journey ahead.

INTRODUCTION

Amidst the intricate design of human experiences, our expectations often diverge from the harsh fabric of reality. More frequently than not, life unfolds in ways we could never have foreseen. Whilst we wield the pen that carves our destinies, there exist aspects of life that are beyond our control. Although life may deal us a seemingly 'unfavourable hand', the Almighty God has graced us with His divine presence, power, and goodness to turn curses into blessings, failures into success, and misfortunes into favour. Regardless of the cards dealt to us, our response to each challenge becomes the fulcrum upon which our desires and fears hinge.

I was not born into privilege, but with age came the realisation that some battles are worth fighting. The essence of this book lies in the constant revelation of the thought that 'It's not where you start, but how you finish'. My encouragement for those who face adversity right at the onset, just as I did, is that there's still an opportunity for a triumphant finish. It is important to emphasise that it's not just about winning but about the lessons you have learnt when you cross the finish line.

This memoir is my humble attempt to unravel the threads of my existence, to trace the steps that have led me to this moment, and to share the remarkable journey that has defined the person I am today. It is a testament to the extraordinary people, places, and pivotal moments that have left an indelible mark on my soul - offering a glimpse into the adventures, triumphs, and trials that have sculpted the narrative of my life.

Many exceptional individuals have been recorded in the annals of history, and I consider myself among them. However, they did not triumph in their early years. Yet, they concluded their journey with remarkable stories and enduring legacies. I think of luminaries such as Thomas Edison, Albert Einstein, Ben Carson, and Jamaican activist Marcus Mosiah Garvey.

As I close this chapter, I do so with purpose and anticipation. The journey is often uncertain, but I am guided by the unshakeable belief that I will achieve greatness like those before me. It is not merely a proclamation but a declaration of my unwavering faith in God's word. The subsequent chapters await, and with each page turned, I step closer to realising my aspirations.

I am the architect of my destiny, and in the tiniest beams of hope, I find the strength to shape a life that resonates with greatness. The story continues, and with each new chapter, I march forward, embracing the extraordinary potential that lies within. Greatness is not a distant mirage; it is the terminus where my destiny lies.

CHAPTER 1

Footprints In Time

ON A WARM SEPTEMBER DAY in 1978 in the Garden Parish of St. Ann, Jamaica, I made my debut into this world, born into the loving embrace of Inez Shaw and Joseph Henlon. The early chapters of my life read like a familiar tale of childhood. With the picturesque backdrop of St. Ann's Bay shaping my formative years, little did I know that this ordinary start would pave the way for an extraordinary journey.

In the early years of my life, I lived with either my mother, father, aunt, or grandmother. Living with my grandmother allowed me a certain freedom, as I would be on the road for the most part with my male cousin, playing marbles, hoisting kites, and going to the river. Those were fun days!

My educational voyage commenced with humble steps as I began my academic journey at the local Infant and Primary schools in St Ann's Bay. My potential began to shine here. In 1992, I was soon blessed with a scholarship from the Ministry of Education to continue my studies at a traditional high school in the hills of Claremont.

The day my mother received the letter, her excitement was palpable. I can still recall her joy as she clutched the letter which held the key to my financial hopes and dreams. However, things turned out differently than she had hoped, as the letter she received was a 'standard notification sent to all students' according to the secretary at the school. Nevertheless, my mother's determination knew no bounds. She would go to great lengths to ensure that each school year, I had all the required books on the reading list.

As I traversed my early years, I often reflected on my experiences as an only child. It sometimes seemed lonesome, but I learned to embrace and cherish that solitude. I would frequently engage in long conversations with myself and immerse myself in the classroom teacher role. In my downtime, I would craft poems and find comfort in sleep. Though mundane, these activities proved to be valuable habits later in life. As I continue to share my story, when and how they benefited me will become more apparent.

As I grew older and started my own family, my story took a humorous twist. I became pregnant with my second child while my mother was pregnant with my brother at the same time. It's a memory that never fails to bring a chuckle. I've shared this anecdote with many, constantly receiving a hearty laugh in response. Sadly, my children didn't find it quite as amusing, as they frequently faced the challenge of explaining the unconventional family dynamics.

Being the eldest of three on my father's side and the only child on my mother's side, I travelled a unique path. I lacked the buffer of an older sibling to offer advice or defend me when bullies lurked. This vulnerability made me an easy target, leading to more than one occasion of being tormented by a group of girls during my primary school days. My soft-spoken nature often made me an easy target, but a turning point came when a boy picked on me and tried to show off his karate skills during lunchtime. I finally mustered the courage to stand up for myself and told him to leave me alone. It was a small victory, but it did little to prepare me for the bullying I again faced as I transitioned from primary school to high school.

Initially, high school was a place of normalcy for me, where I remained reserved and focused on my studies. However, an unfortunate incident almost destroyed my newfound peace. I had always been punctual for school, a habit I deeply valued. But one morning, a boy from my community called me over, and to my horror and disbelief, he slapped me and fled to the rooftop. I was furious. I seriously wanted to teach that boy a lesson but refrained, wanting to uphold my impeccable record. I decided to report the incident instead. However, I was met with indifference, with a dismissive remark urging me to "go to class, [as] rolling stone gathers no moss." I wasn't sure what hurt me more - the lack of support I received from the teacher with whom I sought counsel or the slap I received from the bully.

It was an emotional setback for me. I wondered if people could find any justice in the world. Still, I was determined not to let the boy off the hook. So, I turned to my father for support. He assured me he would take care of the problem, and sure, he did, as that boy never bothered me again. I was happy with the outcome, but it had created enemies, as the girls I once thought were my friends turned against me, citing,

'I should not have reported the incident to my father.' I was crushed but determined not to let it destroy me.

My father was an ex-soldier. He possessed an unconquerable spirit, which significantly influenced my life. He had a strong work ethic with a *soft spot* for the ladies. This characteristic occasionally got the best of him. Despite the occasional tug-of-war between my parents, each vying for my attention, I cherished the memories of my father's presence in my life. Even though our interactions were sporadic, I held a deep affection for him. I proudly wore the title of "Sojie's daughter."

And so, my story began in the quiet parish of St Ann, setting the stage for the twists and turns that would shape my journey. The challenges I faced as a child moulded me into the resilient person I have become, owing to my mother's unwavering support and my father's guiding influence.

CHAPTER 2

A Mother's Care

WOVEN INTO THE FABRIC OF MY EXISTENCE, one thread that stands out prominently is my mother's profound influence. Her commitment to my well-being and education shaped the very fibre of my existence, weaving a narrative of love and sacrifice.

From the earliest days of my childhood, she became the engineer of my dreams, inspiring me to put my best foot forward and accomplish what she did not. She catered to my physical, intellectual, and spiritual growth with hands that held tenderness and resilience. In a world that often felt overwhelming, her unwavering support was a fortress, giving me the courage to confront every hurdle.

She believed education was the key to unlocking endless opportunities. With determination etched into every decision, my mother ensured I attended school and thrived within its walls. Her sacrifice was tangible—from long work hours to late nights spent poring over textbooks with me. She was my beacon of encouragement.

She was my constant ally in the pursuit of academic success. Her tireless support met the challenges of assignments and exams, transforming our home into a sanctuary of learning. Although she knew nothing I had within the covers of my book, her wisdom was a guiding light, steering me through the labyrinth of knowledge with patience and love.

Her impact went beyond textbooks and report cards. She instilled in me values that would become the compass for navigating life's intricate passages. Compassion, resilience, and a relentless pursuit of excellence were not just lessons but the principles etched into the core of my being by a mother who believed in my potential.

Reflecting on the journey, I am confident that my mother's influence extended beyond academics. She has been a silent force, a source of inspiration, and the embodiment of selfless love. Her sacrifices and unwavering commitment have laid the foundation for my aspirations and achievements.

In this short chapter of my life, my mother emerges as the heroine, the driving force behind my growth and success. Through her, I have learned that love and education are intertwined, creating a force that withstands the test of time. Her legacy is not just the marks on a report card but the indelible impressions on my character, forever shaping the woman I am becoming.

CHAPTER 3

Father Figures

Joseph (Sojie) Henlon

JOSEPH HAD AN INDOMITABLE SPIRIT. However, in 2015, his walls came crashing in and shook the foundation of everything he believed in. My father was known to many as a strong, determined soul who could bounce back from any challenge – qualities I believe he developed from his army training. But in 2015, he became seriously ill, and this time around, he was about to fight a battle for which the army could never have prepared him.

At a critical point during his illness, he reached out to me for help, expressing his need to go to the Hospital. Unfortunately, I was unable to accompany him, as I had just been discharged from the Hospital after undergoing surgery. Instead, my daughter accompanied him. My father was later joined by my sister and her mother, who travelled from Kingston to visit and support him during this challenging period. My father's wife, however, could not make the trip due to her incapacitation.

Upon visiting my father for the first time after my health improved, it became evident that his condition was critical. He was unable to take personal care of himself and required oxygen due to the development of sepsis. To make matters worse, he received a diagnosis of non-Hodgkin lymphoma. This cancer originates in the lymphatic system of the body. I remember visiting him one Sunday afternoon. This visit was not the usual. My sister, her mother, and my father's dad, affectionately called Mas' Lambert, accompanied me. The funniest thing about this visit was that my dad made the strangest request. My dad requested Jerked Pork. You heard me right. This request was rather ridiculous as my father did not eat pork. He laughed and said, "It's salty!"

I was appointed the next of kin as my stepmother, my dad's wife, was gravely ill and, therefore, could not care for him. A doctor walked into the room and took me aside. She said, "Your dad has been diagnosed with cancer of the lymph nodes." She cited that persons with the illness usually do not live beyond three months. She continued, "You may visit anytime you wish." This prognosis was grim, as they pronounced he had only three months to live. Tragically, he passed away just three weeks after being transferred to a Kingston-based hospital for further testing and treatment.

The phone call I received on August 14, 2015, will forever be etched in my mind. Nothing I experienced up to that point could have prepared me for his untimely death. He was only 56 years old. He had much for which to live, but the cold hands of death had snatched him away from me. Our last conversation began replaying like a scratched record: "Can't text you, Keisha; my fingers are weak." This conversation was the last time I heard his voice, as on August 13, 2015, he closed his eyes and said goodbye. Despite his short battle with the illness, my father's unconquerable spirit and the memories of his rugged personality will ensure that he will never be forgotten. Seemingly unable to endure the torture of the void left by his departure, his wife followed him into eternity just 13 days later.

Lambert Henlon

Lambert Henlon, the sole grandparent from my father's lineage with whom I had the privilege of spending cherished moments, was a constant presence throughout my childhood. He was one of my caregivers when my father, a dedicated soldier, had to fulfil his duties. Lambert Henlon was pivotal in nurturing and helping shape my formative years.

Thinking about him now, I can remember when I was about six years old, my mother had journeyed from St Mary to have me live with her. But my father would have none of it. They both held either hand, pulling me back and forth. My grandfather was upset over what he saw and pulled me from their grasp. This was never something a child should experience, but this was my reality.

In 2017, life's unstoppable cycle unfolded as my grandfather's health began to falter—the tables again turned. Out of concern for his well-being, I was uncomfortable with the idea of him living alone. So, I invited him to stay at my house. Little did I anticipate that the roles would reverse one day, and I, too, would be tasked with caring for him.

On the fateful morning of April 13, 2017, my grandfather was rushed to the Hospital. As the doctors conducted essential blood work, a brief conversation between us took an unexpected turn. With a profound sense of acceptance, he quietly uttered, "I am not returning home with you." The weight of those words brought tears to my eyes, grappling with the impending departure of a beloved patriarch. Amid this emotional turmoil, he requested a drink of water. As I offered it to him, he sought his medication. I advised him that he had to eat first. His voice then reduced to a whisper, his eyes fixed, and a disturbing stillness settled upon him. Distressed, I summoned a doctor for assistance.

With the assistance of one of his grandnieces, we carefully lifted him onto a gurney as attending doctors initiated CPR. However, my grandfather lay there, unmoving - a silent testament to his departure from this world. Another Henlon, a pillar of my family, had passed. The fact that he was 92 years old still did not prepare me for the void his absence would leave. Worries about his recent series of illnesses had plagued me, particularly as his doctor suspected he had cancer. Yet, it was his beleaguered heart, not the spectre of cancer, that ultimately claimed him. As I grappled with the reality of his passing, memories of Lambert Henlon, a man of strength, love, and familial devotion, will forever be etched in the chambers of my heart.

Steadman

While Joseph Henlon was my biological father, someone else in my life contributed significantly to my success, for whom I am eternally grateful—Steadman, my stepfather.

Mister Lloyd, as I affectionately call him, is the best stepfather any child could have asked for. I cannot recall any instance where he had to raise his voice at me or even administer corporal punishment -He epitomised a good father. He was there throughout my childhood, providing unwavering support as I embarked on and completed my Diploma in Teaching. It's not often that you come across a male figure who takes full responsibility for a child who is not biologically his own. When I sometimes hear about the crimes committed by some stepfathers against their stepchildren, it only deepens my appreciation for the stepfather I have been fortunate to have in my life.

In my formative years, and even to this day, some people refer to him as my father. No one could know that he was not my biological father unless I told them. From nine until I graduated college, he provided the foundation I needed to grow and mature into a strong black woman. He, too, has a daughter, and coincidentally, we both share the same first name - she is Nickeisha, and I am Nikeisha.

In reflecting on my journey, I am profoundly grateful for the pivotal role Steadman played in shaping the person I am today. While Joseph Henlon may have been my biological father, Steadman's steadfast love, support, and guidance throughout my childhood were quite impactful. His presence and genuine care have not only influenced my academic and personal achievements but have also instilled in me the values of commitment and determination. As I move forward in life, I carry with me a profound appreciation for the blessing of having Steadman as not just a stepfather but as a true father figure.

CHAPTER 4

Chronicles Of Resilience

IN 1997, I EMBARKED ON MY COLLEGE JOURNEY, a moment of immense pride for myself and my family. I was the first in my family to attend college, not just any college but Teachers' College. For my mother, this was an even more cherished milestone. She had lived to witness her 'one eye,' as they say in Jamaican vernacular, setting off for Teachers' College. It was a challenging road; however, I did not once lack the essential resources to complete my studies in those three years. My mother worked tirelessly at two jobs to meet my needs, and her sense of pride knew no bounds.

College ushered in a newfound sense of freedom and independence that I had not experienced before. However, with this liberation came a heightened sense of responsibility, which I held in the highest regard. Unlike some of my peers, I would only leave the campus when necessary. Being away from home provided an environment where many different behaviours could flourish. Still, I remained steadfast in upholding the values instilled in me during my upbringing.

Saturdays, for me, were reserved for attending church. After the service, I would return to the campus around midday for a much-needed nap. It was on one such Sabbath day that I had a memorable encounter. As I approached the church entrance, I spotted an individual whose words had once taunted me during high school. She seemed to remember me, although I doubted, she recalled our past encounter. However, I greeted her with a warm smile, spoke briefly, and went on my way. Looking back, I am grateful to God that there was no lingering hatred towards her. The Bible says in Luke 6: 27-28: *"Love your enemies, do good to them which hate you, bless them that curse you, and pray for them which despitefully use you."* - KJV I can see now that her words in high school only motivated and propelled me forward.

The service was memorable, and the singing was excellent. I left at the first opportunity and walked briskly back to the college. The afternoon was quiet as some students had gone to spend the weekend with their families. This was never something I could do as I had to 'pinch' the little money I had and reserve going home only for holiday breaks. College life had its ups and downs, but most importantly, it helped to expand my love for writing – a passion I developed during my childhood. At college, I wrote and published my first poem, and although a friend had lost it, the thought of seeing my name appear in the newspaper was a great accomplishment.

In the year 2000, fresh out of college and facing the responsibilities of a young mother, I was confronted with the harsh reality of a saturated education system. The job market, flooded with recent eager graduates, provided fierce competition. Even those who, like me, completed their Secondary Education found themselves teaching at Primary Schools due to the scarcity of opportunities.

I embarked on my teaching journey as a grade four teacher, a position that was, unfortunately, temporary. The need for permanent employment loomed large, and the job had to be not just any vacancy but a clear, stable position. The Ministry of Education had a system for teachers struggling to secure a job—where you would submit your name to the regional office. This simple action opened the door for me to attend an interview at a school in St Mary, a daily trek of approximately forty miles that cost me more than $20,000 at that time, a significant burden for a young mother and newlywed.

Obtaining a job was a blessing. It is endowed with the extraordinary task of touching and moulding the lives of those entrusted in my care. However, teaching over 500 students within an academic year proved daunting, taking a toll on my emotional, psychological, and spiritual well-being. It was a challenging chapter, marked by extreme stress and the relentless demands of a heavy workload.

Fast-forward to 2015, 14 years into my tenure at this school, a pivotal moment emerged. Following my father's passing and the retirement of the Head of the Business Department, I was promoted to teach grades 10 and 11. It was unfamiliar terrain, but this shift catalysed my aspirations toward becoming a principal.

The initial cohort of students did not perform as expected, and I suspected that the change of teacher and my relative newness to the role contributed to the outcome. Determined to alter the narrative, I committed to an extraordinary work ethic. Late nights became the norm as I worked tirelessly with students to ensure their success in Electronic Document Preparation and Management, Principles of Business, and Office Administration.

My efforts culminated in 2017, when I witnessed a remarkable 100% pass rate in those subjects. My students and I shared the elation, which they proved in a touching gesture by presenting me with a plaque during their graduation ceremony. I had helped them achieve their goals. In return, they made me a proud teacher.

Buoyed by this success, I set my sights on further academic pursuits, and in 2017, I began the journey towards a Master of Education Degree. Initially drawn to Educational Policy and Planning, I pivoted to Educational Measurement as the former was only offered face-to-face. The satisfaction I derived from my current accomplishments and the determination to contribute to education's broader landscape fuelled my pursuit of continuous learning and professional growth.

In the climactic chapter of my master's programme, I embarked on a daring venture, seizing the opportunity to enrol in the prestigious college for Aspiring Principals and Educational Leaders. With an unwavering determination to make an indelible mark on the education system, I committed myself to a journey of profound significance. The path ahead may be arduous, but my resolve is unbendable. I am prepared to await the transformative impact I aim to unleash patiently.

CHAPTER 5

Never Give Up

UNRELENTING CHALLENGES MARKED MY JOURNEY, but the thought of giving up never crossed my mind. For 18 years, I toiled away from my home parish. This choice took a heavy toll on my finances, my family, and my spiritual, emotional, and psychological well-being. People often questioned why I persisted in such circumstances; they saw me as brave, but they couldn't fathom my paralysing fear of venturing from the familiar into the unknown.

I yearned to be with my two children, but my relentless pursuit of helping to put food on the table and shoes on their feet meant that I had to miss many precious moments with them. I was merely doing what I had to, with no alternative. Children require material support, but offering them love and emotional sustenance is far more valuable. As many young mothers do, I, too, fell into the trap of thinking that as long as they had food and shelter, they would be fine.

I still vividly recall the days I worked at this shift school. The morning shift required me to rise as early as 2 or 3 a.m. to make it to St. Mary by 6 a.m. My children were fast asleep during those periods, so I would be long gone for work by the time they got up. I would return home after a long day of commuting across parishes, with just enough time to steal precious moments of rest before cooking dinner and welcoming my children back from school.

My family was significantly affected by these events. My children were not getting the love and support they needed, and neither was my husband. There were no family outings or get-togethers, no eating with the family around the dining table, or even worship at the family altar. I simply had no time. Schoolwork consumed my life—from lesson plans and tests to preparing students for CSEC examinations and marking SBAs. I had a difficult time balancing it all.

When the shifts changed, the nightmare of being an absentee mother didn't improve. Afternoon shifts often saw me arriving home as late as 8 p.m. after my children were already in bed. On top of all of that, my health suffered immensely, primarily when I was assigned to work across shifts. By 2005, I was grappling with Acid Reflux disease and desperately in need of medical care. The disease forced me to eat in small portions every two hours to avoid excruciating pain and involuntary expulsions.

As my health deteriorated, my walls began to crumble around me, disrupting my daily routines. In my quest to find a solution, I had over two years visited fifteen (15) different medical practitioners, including a gastroenterologist, hoping to find an effective treatment. One April morning, overwhelmed by reflux episodes, I contemplated the unthinkable – death. Clad for work but too unwell to leave, I cried out to God. At that moment, His spirit whispered to me the words Job once spoke: "*And though after my skin worms destroy this body, yet in my flesh shall I see God;" – KJV (Job 19:26).* In my darkest hour, God filled me with hope, reassuring me that He had not abandoned me.

I heard the words spoken to David in the Psalms, "*And call upon Me in the day of trouble; I will deliver you, and you will honour Me." – KJV (Psalm 50:15).* After this spiritual encounter, I felt a renewed sense of purpose. I found the strength that I needed to go on.

My husband was ready to take me to the Hospital. As I went, I prayed to God, as I was at my wits and needed a solution. I met a doctor as I walked into a small room at the Regional Hospital. He listened attentively to my story. Then, with a reassuring smile, he prescribed a medication that had been proven effective for other patients like me. He said, "Let's try it and see if it helps."

I gradually returned to my former self. For over five years, I continued taking the medication, fearing a relapse if I stopped. But by 2010, I felt a profound change. My health had improved to the extent that I became pregnant, and I had no stomach-related problems. I thank God for guiding me, and I am now entirely free from that medication. This journey was arduous, but I emerged more robust and resilient than ever.

CHAPTER 6

Finding Hope After Miscarriage

IN 2013, I WENT INTO PREMATURE LABOUR at five (5) months and gave birth to a son I called Raymond. This miscarriage would be the second time that I would be losing a son. In the year before that, I suffered a miscarriage at three (3) months. For years, I was devastated but never sought counselling. I told myself that I could handle it on my own. Ideally, whatever I had to do in order not to think about it was what I did. If engulfing myself with work was the pull, I was willing to take it.

This was how I felt then, but looking back at it now, it would have been a recipe for disaster had I not decided to accept the hand life had dealt me and to be more intentional about navigating the negative emotions.

So, after two failed attempts, I did more rigorous health checks to understand what was happening to my body. Finally, I was diagnosed with a condition known as Endometriosis, which proved to be the source of my miscarriages. The ordeal was a lot to handle. When it rains, it pours! That was how I felt. Still, I was not willing to give up just yet. God always has the final say.

Having these miscarriages was no ordinary ordeal, for I had already been through the horrifying experience of having my cervix stitched up months in advance in an attempt to retain my pregnancies. Still, it was as if fate itself had conspired against me.

In that dimly lit room, I could feel the excruciating tension in the air as the attending doctor grappled with the unfamiliar terrain of my body. The sensation of searing pain coursed through me, but I clung to a fragile hope that this, too, would eventually pass. In that harrowing moment, I held on to the belief that amidst the darkest hours, there was a glimmer of light, a promise that, perhaps, the storm would eventually subside.

Within minutes of removing the sutures that had once held the child in, he was out into a world for which he was ill-prepared, and within minutes, he departed from me. I was devastated. I had lost a second son, a son I so desperately needed. I cried myself to sleep as I watched other mothers cuddle their babies on their beds beside me. This was new and scary. My life was ruled by fear - fear of what else could go wrong.

I found myself crying within the first two years of their passing. Yet, amidst the pain and uncertainty, a resilient spirit emerges, reminding me that adversity can catalyse growth. Although marked by profound challenges, this chapter of my life is not defined solely by loss; it is a testament to finding strength in vulnerability.

As I navigated the complexities of my journey, I found solace in the possibility of raising awareness, fostering empathy, and forging connections with others who share similar struggles. Through sharing my story, I aim to transform the narrative, turning pain into purpose and fostering a sense of community that transcends the boundaries of Endometriosis.

Today, God has blessed me with three (3) exceptional children: Onielia, Elizabeth, and Joelle. I am delighted to have them in my life.

CHAPTER 7

When Life Throws You Lemons...

WHEN LIFE THROWS YOU LEMONS, it is easy to get discouraged and lose sight of your dreams. My journey had been far from what I envisioned back in 2004. At that time, the Chairman of the School where I was employed had inspired us to set goals for the next five years. At that time, my five-year plan included pursuing a Bachelor of Education Degree at a University in Kingston and advancing to becoming a school's headmistress. But little did I know that the road ahead would have challenges and disappointments. I often found comfort in one of my favourite original quotes:

> *"Disappointments are like 'sleeping police'; they slow you down, but don't let them stop you."*
>
> **- *Nikeisha Henlon-Sterling***

Over the next fifteen years, I dedicated myself to academic and professional development, driven by a strong desire to make a difference in students' lives. The high number of illiterate students who were graduating from high school, often without valuable skills for the future, disheartened me. It was during this journey that I decided to pursue a Master of Education Degree in Educational Measurement at a prominent University in the city of Kingston. My mission was to advocate for functionally illiterate students, ensuring they had an equal opportunity to demonstrate their knowledge without the burden of written tests.

In 2019, I attended a training college for aspiring principals. I was determined to use this platform to drive the change I passionately believed in. My focus was finding alternative ways to certify functionally illiterate students without subjecting them to written exams. I reached out and shared my vision, but sadly, it was met with discouragement. Even though I couldn't bring about the change I longed for, I still hoped it would happen someday.

Life led me on an unexpected path, and I had to adapt to new challenges, especially concerning my health. This path forced me to consider the 'what if' scenario – what if I can no longer work? I decided to invest in skill-based courses as my Plan B, ensuring I have options if my health disrupts my regular work schedule. Despite the challenges I had with my health, I managed to pursue a Bachelor of Science Degree in Accounting. This decision had not been without its detractors. Yet, I recall the words of the great Marcus Mosiah Garvey, who once said, *'Never stop reading,'* and, by extension, one should never stop learning. My journey continues as I strive to make a meaningful impact, no matter the obstacles life throws me. I ultimately want to leave a legacy for my children. Another expression I use to encourage myself is:

> *"When God has equipped you with what you need to know, He will lead you to places you will need to go."*
> ***– Nikeisha Henlon-Sterling***

CHAPTER 8

Time For A Change

IN THE TUMULTUOUS YEAR OF 2020, amid the relentless grip of the pandemic, an unwavering determination surged within me. Tethered to a school in St Mary for 18 long years, but the time had come for a seismic change. The uncertainty that once held me captive was now obliterated by an uncompromising realisation that staying was no longer an option.

My body, weathered by an arduous daily commute, could no longer endure the strain, and the magnetic pull of family drew me closer. My children, aged 20, 17, and 10, needed my presence to be felt, and I, too, yearned to be an integral part of their lives.

Pursuing a new chapter, I contacted a trusted friend employed at a high school in St Ann. Through her encouragement, I took a leap of faith and applied for work at this institution. The interview, a crucible of exhaustion, witnessed my best efforts, but success eluded me. In the wake of this setback, I found myself standing at the crossroads, questioning the trajectory of my life.

In moments of profound introspection, I turned to prayer, seeking divine guidance. With sincerity of heart, I implored the Lord to pave the way for a job closer to home. I posited that my body could no longer endure the gruelling 80-mile daily commute and pleaded for an answer.

About a week after that, my phone rang. As fate would have it, the school that initially deemed me unsuccessful now offered me a job. I was left flabbergasted! I struggled to comprehend the words. In disbelief, I expressed gratitude for the unexpected turn of events and ended the call. The force of change, propelled by my unwavering determination, affirmed that sometimes, against all odds, persistence and prayer can carve a path where none seemed to exist.

CHAPTER 9

Conquering The Silence

IN 2023, MY LIFE TOOK A DRASTIC TURN when I received a life-altering diagnosis that would reshape my world. Obstructive Sleep Apnea, a condition I had never given much thought to before, became a formidable adversary. The haunting awareness that, within an hour, I would experience up to thirty events in which I would either stop breathing or have very shallow breathing held me captive in a realm of fear. Coupled with Osteo-Arthritis, it was a double blow that knocked me off my feet, both literally and metaphorically. I never thought that at 45, I would struggle to move about freely or even kneel to pray.

There were days when the simple task of getting out of bed seemed a monumental struggle. The fatigue was overwhelming, and I couldn't understand why. Mere survival seemed like an insurmountable challenge during those periods of my life.

As I would soon learn, Obstructive Sleep Apnea is a condition in which a person's breathing stops during sleep, only to be jolted awake by the brain's desperate attempt to restore respiration. It is a silent predator that strikes when you least expect it, robbing you of the peaceful, restorative sleep your body craves.

I employed a myriad of treatments, hoping that medications would clear my sinuses and bring relief. I believed I was on the path to recovery, but it soon became evident that the battle was far from over. I began experiencing persistent daytime sleepiness, even after what felt like a full night's rest. It was like a relentless fog that clouded my every waking moment. Falling asleep at work, nodding off while driving, struggling to concentrate, and forgetting simple things became part of my daily life. Being alert had become a luxury I could no longer afford.

Ironically, during this trying time, I was pursuing a Culinary Arts course at a Culinary School in Jamaica. The culinary world was another passion of mine, and I was determined to excel. Yet, my condition threatened to shatter my dreams, and only my family was privy to my hidden pain.

I knew that I had greatness within me, and I was determined to find a way to conquer this relentless foe. The persistent exhaustion, the coughing fits after drifting off, the interrupted sleep throughout the night, and the dangerous moments behind the wheel all became unbearable.

My newfound independence, marked by my success in driving my car, was snatched away just nine months after its purchase, as my doctor reiterated the words: “Do not drive.” Once again, walking, the very thing I had tried so hard to escape, was forced upon me. The pain of Osteoarthritis gripped my legs, and my back tightened, but I was grateful to be blessed with a supportive husband and co-workers.

The physical pain was only part of the story. My condition began to seep into my personal life, undermining my emotional and mental well-being. On a scale from 1 to 10, my libido plummeted to zero. I descended into the depths of depression - a secret I kept hidden from the world. I excelled at work, motivated others, empowered my children, and maintained an active social media presence while silently suffering. I wrestled with feelings of inadequacy, wondering if my husband believed I was no longer attracted to him or perceived me as lazy. It was a dark period of internal conflict and pain.

As usual, I found the courage to motivate myself by turning to my faith, drawing strength from my favourite passage of Scripture: 1 Samuel 30:6. "*And David was greatly distressed...but David encouraged himself in the Lord his God.*" – KJV Just as David found solace in God's word during his trials, I sought refuge in my faith, believing that God had a purpose for me even amid my suffering.

My husband's simple encouragement to "worship" brought a turning point. I realised I had been complaining and not worshipping. I had allowed my circumstances to define me rather than lifting myself and drawing strength from my faith. I knew God could turn my life around, but I had to come to terms with His timing, which differed from mine. The accolades and achievements that had once defined me were irrelevant in the face of the transformative shift that awaited me.

Sleep Apnea had invaded my life, bringing a myriad of challenges and tribulations. But I was determined to find my strength and purpose once more, to rise above my circumstances, and to inspire others to do the same. My journey through this chapter of my life was far from over, but I was ready to face it head-on with unwavering faith and determination.

CHAPTER 10

The Journey To Find Sleep

IMAGINE THE FEELING OF EXHAUSTION weighing you down night after night. Endless hours spent tossing and turning, with infinite thoughts and worries racing through your mind. Sleep - that elusive treasure slipping through your grasp, and you are powerless to stop it. It is a plight that few can relate to and one I would not wish for others to experience.

On September 7, 2023, I embarked on a journey to seek comfort and to find answers to my sleepless nights. My destination: Kingston, a city of hope, and within it, a Seventh-Day Adventist Hospital. The moment I walked through those doors, I was met with warmth and compassion that felt like a soothing balm to my restless soul.

I arrived hours before my appointment in a bundle of nerves and fatigue. To my surprise, I was not met with impatience or indifference but with open arms and a welcoming smile. The specialist's office staff made me feel like a cherished guest rather than just another patient. Their kindness and exceptional customer service deeply moved me.

Then came the moment I met the Sleep Specialist – a doctor with a heartwarming smile that instantly put me at ease. He didn't just treat me as another medical case but as a person with struggles, fears, and pains. The conversation started casually, allowing me to open up as if talking to an old friend. It was as though he had a window into my soul, understanding even the silent cries for help building up within me.

He knew about those moments when I had considered quitting my job, overwhelmed by the constant fatigue and inability to manage my daily life. His empathy and understanding were a lifeline in that moment, a ray of hope I so desperately needed.

As our conversation unfolded over an hour, it became clear that I wasn't alone in this battle for a good night's sleep. The doctor didn't just offer me words of reassurance; he provided a solution, a device that would help diagnose the extent to which Sleep Apnea disrupted my sleep.

The first night with the device went less smoothly than I had hoped. The exhaustion from the countless sleepless nights had taken its toll, and I was too tired to begin the test. But I made a vow to myself: 'I will conquer this sleepless monster'. I had to find a way to regain my peaceful nights and get that much-needed rest before facing the challenges of a new day, even if it meant enduring the uncertainty of the night.

My journey to this Hospital was not just a visit to a medical facility but a journey of hope and understanding. It was a reminder that there are people who genuinely care and are dedicated to helping you find the answers you so desperately seek. So, to all those who have battled sleepless nights and restless minds, I want you to know that you are not alone, and there is hope for a better night's sleep just around the corner.

CHAPTER 11

Finding Strength In Adversity

I WAS IN AGONY. My heart was heavy. The physical pain and the weight of uncertainty were unbearable. One morning, at around 4 a.m., dark clouds of doom cast a heavy shroud over my thoughts. I desperately cried out to God, my voice cracking insufferably: "Help me, Lord!"

I got up to relieve myself, and as I shuffled towards the bathroom, my knees protested with every step. I felt like a fragile vessel, one misstep away from a humiliating accident. Under the cascading water from the shower, I couldn't help but wonder about the future. What prospects lie ahead for me? As I pondered, my mind became clouded with exhaustion that seemed to have settled in my bones. Unfinished tasks and unread notes loomed over me, casting shadows of despair on my aspirations. The burden of it all threatened to break my spirit, and a sudden, overwhelming urge to give up washed over me like an icy wave.

Every movement was an ordeal, each step a battle against the relentless pain. The simple act of getting in and out of a car felt like climbing a mountain. Doubts crept in, like a haunting whisper in my mind, telling me that I might never finish my Accounting Degree. It was as if a cruel, disembodied voice was prophesying my failure.

But then, amidst the turmoil, questions arose: If I lacked the will to persevere, what message would it send to those who doubted me? Or to those who questioned my strength and determination? What words of inspiration could I offer those who found their courage in my relentless pursuit of my dreams?

Out of nowhere, as I stood in the shower that morning, a well-known gospel song suddenly filled my mind. I began to sing the lyrics I knew by heart, letting the powerful, soul-stirring words wash over me like a healing stream:

"Take me to the King
I don't have much to bring
My heart's torn in pieces
It's my offering
Lay me at the throne
Leave me there alone
To gaze upon Your glory
And sing to You this song..."
- *Tamela Mann*

I was at the intersection of despair and hope in that vulnerable moment. The weight of my struggles threatened to crush me, but the flicker of determination burned within. These lyrics became my anthem, a reminder that even in the face of pain and uncertainty, my spirit could find solace and strength through the power of faith and determination.

In these moments of agony, the human spirit's resilience shone brightest. The pain and doubt were real, but so was my unwavering resolve to defy the odds. I often tell myself, Nikeisha, "Follow in the momentum that drives your spirit to excel; seize the moment and capture every opportunity", – and that is precisely what I did.

I clung to that anthem through the haze of exhaustion and uncertainty, letting it resonate in my soul. It was a lifeline, a reminder that God's grace is immeasurable and that with Him, I can weather even the darkest storms. During my turmoil, I discovered a profound truth: faith and determination can pierce through the deepest shadows, and we can find the strength to carry on in the midst of the most profound suffering. I live by the conviction that:

> "The only 'No' you should accept is the one that sets 'No Limit' on you!"
> – ***Nikeisha Henlon-Sterling***

So, as the water washed over me, I sang those lyrics with all the strength my body could muster. I knew that I was not alone in my struggle. My journey was not just about me; it was a testament to God's ability to empower and equip the human spirit with the resilience it needs to survive and overcome. In sharing this story, I could offer a glimmer of hope to those facing their battles: a reminder that even in the darkest moments, the flame of determination can light the way forward.

CHAPTER 12

Reflection: Strength In Adversity

AS I CONTEMPLATE THE PATH I'VE TRAVELLED, I can vividly recall the countless moments I found myself in the depths of emotional despair. Yet, I consistently summoned the strength to present my best self to the world. Even in those challenging times, I would craft small yet potent motivational quotes, which I shared with many. People say that 'you cannot give from an empty well', but the responses I received refilled my reservoir and enabled me always to have enough to spare.

I grappled with persistent feelings of doubt and worthlessness, particularly when I struggled to contribute to the well-being of my family and even myself. Nevertheless, one thing that remained unwavering was 'hope'. Yes, there were instances when hope seemed distant and moments when I second-guessed my ability to complete a Master's Degree, wishing I had opted for a skills training course instead. Failure, however, was never an option for me. I needed to be a pillar of strength for my daughters and those who regarded me as their role model. I sincerely believe that:

> *"Our greatest strength lies in our ability to exercise resilience in the midst of adversity."*
> ***– Nikeisha Henlon-Sterling***

Jeremiah 29:11 became my guiding light during my darkest hours. Life's reality is that we navigate a physical world influenced by negative and positive forces. I am sure that I should not have survived the numerous spiritual assaults directed my way, but then came God. But God...

The emotions that had quietly resided within me, concealed by the years of toil spent away from my roots, were resurfacing. They crept back into my consciousness, their presence undeniable. It became increasingly evident that I could no longer accomplish the tasks I once effortlessly managed. Once my ally, time was now a relentless foe, slipping through my fingers like fine sand. The reality of my limitations weighed heavily on me, a stark reminder of the changes that had unfolded in my life.

> *"Fear can cripple your ability to achieve your true potential."*
> ***– Nikeisha Henlon-Sterling***

I often reminded myself of this. Hence, I fought hard against the spirit of fear.

One evening, as I sat at the computer, the weight of unfinished schoolwork bore down on me. My husband had inquired about our evening plans; his voice tinged with exhaustion as he yearned for rest. I sensed disappointment when I expressed my need to complete my school assignments. A profound ache settled within me, for I longed to be beside him in our shared haven, to embrace the warmth of our togetherness. In the quiet of that moment, I pondered my predicament. Should I abandon this work, though it was long overdue? Should I make use of the opportunity to reconnect with my husband, who has been suffering from neglect?

The demands of academia had become an unforgiving taskmaster, pulling me deeper into a world of deadlines and obligations. The constant struggle to balance my educational pursuits with the embrace of my personal life had worn me thin like a threadbare tapestry. The cracks in the delicate balance I had tried so hard to maintain had grown irreparable. But I reminded myself:

> *"Do not entertain the spirit of hopelessness; the presence of life is your gift of opportunity."*
> ***– Nikeisha Henlon-Sterling***

In the quiet dawn of a challenging morning, I sought solace and strength in the sacred verses of the Bible. Battling through the labyrinth of financial uncertainties surrounding the publication of this book, I yearned for a divine sign. As I delved into the pages of Proverbs 24, a spiritual revelation unfolded before me—Proverbs 24:10 (KJV): *'If thou faint in the day of adversity, thy strength is small.'* At that moment, I prayed, "Lord, I acknowledge the vastness of my heart and maintain unwavering confidence that triumph awaits. Grant me the fortitude to trust the unfolding journey that leads to victory. Amen!"

Today I affirm:

> *"I smile because I know that there is no mountain in my life that is insurmountable. I am me! I live life knowing that every step that I take has a ripple effect for what is within my purpose."*
> ***- Nikeisha Henlon-Sterling***

CHAPTER 13

Defying The Odds

IN THE FACE OF DISAPPROVAL, my decision to pursue an Accounting Degree became a powerful testament to my resilience. The journey, marked by academic pressures and the weight of discouragement, fuelled an unwavering determination to succeed against all odds. Every obstacle, from the educational challenges to the shadow of Sleep Apnea, became a crucible to test my resolve.

As I faced the daunting prospect of an impending accounting quiz, the pressure intensified, compounded by the relentless demands of academic pursuit and the insidious effects of Sleep Apnea. Yet, the challenges that sought to deter me only strengthened my commitment. Sleep Apnea, with its debilitating side effects, took its toll on me, but I confronted each day with unwavering perseverance.

The turning point was one particular Sunday morning when I decided to acquire a CPAP (Continuous Positive Airway Pressure) machine. As I journeyed into the city with anticipation, I reflected on the distance travelled, the pain endured, and the obstacles I overcame. The treatability of Obstructive Sleep Apnea became a source of gratitude and a testament to the strength of facing adversity head-on. While the battle with Osteoarthritis looms, I rise like a Phoenix, undeterred by the challenges ahead. This machine was a beacon of hope, a symbol of a new lease on life.

Amid it all, the words of Psalm 118:17 echoed within me, reaffirming my resolve to live and declare the words of the Lord. This challenging year has been a crucible of transformation, where every challenge has forged a stronger, more resilient version of myself. In the face of disapproval, academic pressures, and health battles, I've not just finished what I started; I've emerged victorious, a testament to the power of determination, faith, and the indomitable human spirit. I remember that:

> *"Winning does not always mean that you are first in line; it means that you have finished what you had started."*
> **- *Nikeisha Henlon-Sterling***

CHAPTER 14

Redefining Myself

WE OFTEN FIND OURSELVES HOPING, thinking, and feeling our way forward, constantly yearning for a brighter tomorrow. This year, more than ever, I resolved not to leave my success to chance or mere resolutions. I intended to be purposeful in all I did, ensuring that my aspirations didn't remain mere wishes but turned into tangible realities. If my future was going to improve, it was up to me to take deliberate actions to make it happen. It's crucial to understand that:

> *"Disappointments are like temporary roadblocks, slowing us down but never stopping us completely. I refused to let them deter me."*
> **– Nikeisha Henlon-Sterling**

Some of the world's greatest inventions were born out of desperate situations. As Albert Einstein once said, *"Insanity is doing the same thing over and over and expecting different results."* When things do not go our way, there's often the temptation to try multiple approaches. But the truth is, doing everything isn't feasible. We should dedicate time to the one thing that truly matters, the one thing that captures our hearts – our passions and our vision for ourselves.

Have you ever reached a point when you felt like giving up? You felt as if all hope had abandoned you? That's how I felt when I found myself in a deep financial and health crisis, seemingly without a way out.

There were days when I cried and prayed, and then there were days when I couldn't muster the strength to pray. But when I did, it felt like I was having a casual conversation with God. I would say, "God, I know You are all-powerful. I know You can change my situation instantly, but I can't fathom why nothing seems to work for me." To make matters worse, I began second-guessing myself. I felt unaccomplished.

One day, when overwhelmed by the stagnation of my circumstances, my husband received a call, and the caller on the other end asked, "Can you build a house for me?" I could not help but wonder why I wasn't receiving opportunities like that. Little did I know that God had plans for me that would result in a divine shift in my life, turning my dark moments into a life of growth and spiritual prosperity. The writing of this book was the first step in that shift.

It's difficult to see a silver lining behind a dark cloud when nothing seems to work, and every endeavour appears to be met with failure. I remember one Tuesday night, at about

10:34 p.m., I started feeling completely hopeless about my future, as my pursuit of higher education had significantly impacted my income, forcing me to accumulate more debt to pay off existing ones. It was as if I was drowning. But giving up was not an option. If there was a way out, I was determined to find it. I began to comfort myself with the words God spoke into my spirit:

> *"Smile in the midst of disappointments; truth be told, where you want to go may not be where God wants to take you."*
> ***– Nikeisha Henlon-Sterling***

My first step was to acquire a new skill. I felt utterly worthless with a Master's Degree and could barely make ends meet. After sharing my desire to learn a skill with a co-worker, she encouraged me to inquire about short courses offered at a hospitality and training college in the parish.

In 2022, I proudly received a Level 2 Baker (Commis Chef) NVQ-J certificate. However, I knew this was just the beginning. Diagnosed with Osteoarthritis and dealing with two herniated discs in my back, I realised that this could affect my ability to work. It was already painful for me to climb stairs, get in and out of taxis, and even get out of bed. I was frequently late to work due to the physical challenges I faced. But, just like a determined movie character seeking revenge, I reminded myself that it wasn't over until it was over. Life experiences have taught me that:

> *"Transforming self does not require that you start over, but requires that you identify where you are at, and start from there."*
> **– Nikeisha Henlon-Sterling**

I knew that God was more than capable of helping me through this from a spiritual perspective. Yet, from a human standpoint, I needed to push myself, bolstered by faith and confidence in God's ability. As the scripture says, *"Faith without works is dead ..."* Therefore, I convinced myself that if I were to overcome my debt, I had first to redefine who I was.

I completed the baker's course and took on the challenge of enrolling in a Culinary Arts programme at a culinary school in Kingston. While at this institution, I encountered an exceptional instructor who became both a mentor and a source of inspiration. These experiences demonstrated my resilience and opened unexpected doors to new opportunities. I had set out to write my affirmation for the year 2023. I wanted to start the New Year with a new way of thinking but was unwilling to leave it to chance. The following chapters will guide you into building an affirmation for yourself. Always remember:

> *"Today is a new day; embrace it, like never before: live, love, laugh..."*
> **– Nikeisha Henlon-Sterling**

Chapter 15

Transformation

I BEGAN MY TRANSFORMATION with a powerful affirmation. As you enter a new season of your life, I invite you to join me on this journey of self-discovery and personal growth. Like many of us, I made resolutions year after year, hoping for a miraculous transformation. Yet, I realised that real change starts from within. It's time to take control of my life and shape my destiny.

Here's my affirmation for the year 2023:

I am Nikeisha Henlon-Sterling, and I am intentional in all that I do.
I am confident in my ability to achieve what God has in His plan for me.
I love myself and all that God has given me.

My spirit is well, my body is healthy, and I am wealthy.
My mind is sober, and I am not easily angered.
I will walk as God would have me walk daily. I am His, and He is mine.
I can achieve greatness, and I will!

I would repeat it as often as I could remember and even used it as a screen saver to constantly remind me of who I am.

This affirmation was a turning point in my life. It has become the foundation upon which I build my future. It shaped my self-care routines and guided my spiritual journey. Moreover, this affirmation was my compass, pointing me towards financial freedom.

This affirmation transformed my thought processes, making me acutely self-aware. Every action I took was deliberate, and I was now in control of my destiny. As we embark on this transformative journey, remember that your affirmation is the first step in redefining yourself. Embrace it, and let it guide you towards the life you deserve.

> Learn to *"Rise above every situation that makes you feel less than who God has made you to be."*
> ***– Nikeisha Henlon-Sterling***

CHAPTER 16

Who Am I?

THE SCRIPTURE SAYS THERE IS POWER IN THE TONGUE, and I fully comprehend the weight of these words. My name, Nikeisha Henlon-Sterling, is not just a combination of letters but a proclamation of my identity, purpose, and destiny. Every syllable has an inherent power waiting to be unleashed into the universe.

I am Nikeisha Henlon-Sterling, and I declare this with unwavering certainty. I carry within me a unique favour, a divine blessing bestowed upon me from the very moment I took my first breath. I am not here by chance; I am here because I am destined for greatness. I was born to fulfil a God-given purpose, and this purpose is intricately woven into the fabric of my name.

Understanding the significance of my name is the first step on this incredible journey. My name is not a random assortment of letters but a divine assignment. It carries the weight of generations before me and the hopes of future generations. Every syllable resonates with purpose, and God carefully chose every consonant and vowel to define my identity. I understood that my name is not just a word; it is a magnet, attracting that which aligns with my purpose and repelling that which seeks to hinder my progress.

As I embrace my name, I understand that it reflects who I am and who I am to become. My name is a beacon of light, a testament to my unique gifts and talents, and a reminder of the path destined for me.

Knowing the power of my name, I recognised the importance of the company I keep and the energies I allow to associate with it. I will surround myself with positivity, with those who uplift and encourage me on my journey. I guard my name against negativity and influences that seek to diminish its brilliance.

With every word I spoke, I breathed life into the power of my name. With every action I took, I aligned myself with my purpose. I walk this path confidently and determined, knowing that I, Nikeisha Henlon-Sterling, am uniquely favoured and destined to impact the world profoundly.

My name is my declaration, my mission, and my destiny. I embrace it wholeheartedly and am ready to write this powerful chapter of my life.

My dear friends... As you continue to read, think about who you are. Think about what propels you to go forward amidst the daily challenges. These are the things that define you. They are the bedrock of your identity and the soil of your uniqueness.

CHAPTER 17

I Am Intentional

EVERY STEP I TOOK, EVERY DECISION I MADE, was infused with purpose. I had an unwavering intention behind every action, for I understood that to achieve my dreams, I had to pursue them actively. The days of idleness were behind me; I was determined to chase my aspirations with unwavering conviction. I firmly believed that the path God had laid out for me awaited, and unless I dared to step onto that path, I'd never reach my full potential. Failure was not an option; every interview and job offer held the promise of success.

But my belief went beyond mere reliance on external opportunities. I knew that while it's great for someone to extend a helping hand, it's even more empowering to be the one to lift yourself. Recognising your true calling is the cornerstone of all your endeavours. I had found mine and, in response, deliberately curated my life. Everything was a calculated step toward fulfilling my divine destiny, from the friendships I nurtured to the places I ventured, from the conversations in which I engaged to the programmes I instituted.

No longer did I passively wait for destiny to unfold; I had evolved from a 'will happen' mentality to a 'must happen' mindset. Every action I took, every person I engaged with, and every source of assistance I sought were all integral parts of my intentional reality. I'd become an active influencer of the change I longed to see, no longer content to be a passive bystander.

In this chapter of my life, intention was the guiding light that illuminated my path, and the power to manifest my dreams was firmly within my grasp. I had to remind myself that:

> *"Success does not always appear as a signpost; sometimes it is a concealed entrance: you have to look long enough to see it."*
> ***– Nikeisha Henlon-Sterling***

My dear friends... We will never achieve things in life if we stand idly by and let them slip away from us. I learnt pretty early in my life that I was not born wealthy, and as such, I knew that I would have to create wealth for myself and my family. Because life is short and uncertain, we must couple everything we do with reason. If you are to give of yourself, something should come back with your name on it.

> *"Do not be alarmed by failures; no one has ever reached the top before first starting at the bottom!"*
> ***– Nikeisha Henlon-Sterling***

CHAPTER 18

I Am Confident

SELF-CONFIDENCE IS NOT something we were born with but is something we develop as we pursue life. The parable of the talents found in Matthew 25 v 14 -30 (KJV) indicates that God always gives us a start. We were all given a gift - something that we use to glorify God. As I grew and evolved as an Educator, I realised I did very well in motivating others. My first revelation came when I was asked to speak at a principal's banquet in honour of Top Achieving Students in 2014. At the end of the presentation, I was impressed by the feedback I got from teachers.

In 2019, I enrolled at a training institution designed for Aspiring Principals and School Leaders. One of the courses I had to take was 'Transformational Leadership'. This course caused a metamorphosis in my life from a shy, introverted individual to a confident, resilient 'go-getter'. I was no longer afraid to project myself, as I wanted everyone I encountered to know who I was. I did so without hesitation at every opportunity I got. The same year, one of my co-workers at the school based in St. Mary recommended me to a Church pastor to speak at their 'Parent Week' seminar. Once again, I received commendations.

In 2021, I embarked on a transformative journey of self-empowerment; I thought I would love to speak at a school leaving ceremony. To make this dream a reality, I decided to make a deliberate attempt. I subsequently called a former college mate and friend who was also a school principal. I shared with her my desire to speak at her school leaving ceremony, and with great exhilaration, she accepted. The experience was rewarding, and I knew from there that my life would never be the same again.

"If you have no confidence in self, you are twice defeated in the race of life. With confidence, you have won before you have started" - Marcus Mosiah Garvey

My dear friends... Confidence is the belief that no matter what challenges confront you, there is a will deep inside that will conquer them.

CHAPTER 19

I Love Myself

MANY INDIVIDUALS MERELY EXIST. They wake up each day without a profound spiritual purpose. The true essence of self-love manifests in how we care for ourselves. Reflecting on the past, I recall moments when I harboured guilt for pausing due to illness and pushing myself to work even in the face of sickness. During one of my pregnancies, grappling with asthma-related episodes, I neglected seeking medical attention, fearing the consequences of being absent from work.

In an act of self-neglect, I went home that evening, informing a co-worker that I would seek medical attention. I rushed to the hospital, where I was treated and deemed unfit to resume work the next day. At that moment, I jeopardised not only my health but also that of my unborn child.

My infant was later diagnosed with asthma at two years old. While her condition has improved over the years, my life bore witness to countless Hospital visits and sleepless nights. Loving oneself must transcend mere sentiment; it requires deliberate action and an unyielding will to live. Self-love compels conscious decisions about lifestyle, spiritual health, the company we keep, the energies we attract, and our professional aspirations.

My dear friends... True love necessitates first developing a profound love for oneself. This love becomes the impetus for setting boundaries, establishing expectations for acceptable behaviour, and fostering a life guided by self-respect and well-being.

CHAPTER 20

My Spirit Is Well

WE CAN ACHIEVE NOTHING WITHOUT God's divine presence in our aspirations. As the Scripture reminds us in Philippians 4:13 (KJV), *"I can do all things through Christ which strengtheneth me."* This powerful verse serves as a beacon of hope and resilience, a testament to our boundless potential when guided by faith.

In my journey, I found solace and strength through the Word of God. Battling with a myriad of illnesses often left me feeling disheartened and unfulfilled, with the tangible evidence of my physical struggles being ever-present. In those trying moments, I turned to the sacred scriptures, using them as sources of life-affirming energy. I understood that while I may not have been in perfect physical health or financial abundance, I could still boldly declare the promise found in

Romans 4:17 (KJV), which beckons us to *"... call those things which are not as though they were."*

It is crucial to recognise that the absence of worldly success does not equate to the absence of God. Often, we mistakenly attribute life's setbacks to our shortcomings or feel we have been deserted by the divine. Let me assure you today that God is omnipresent, never taking a leave of absence. Consider the profound story of Lazarus, which stands as a testament to God's unwavering presence and the boundless potential for transformation.

Life's existence in this world is a resounding testament to the Almighty's ever-present grace and benevolence. It is a testament to His continuous love and guidance, a reminder that even in our most challenging moments, His divine light shines brightly, offering hope, strength, and the promise of a brighter tomorrow.

My dear friends... Today, I declare that life is a testament to God's everlasting presence. God's essence is woven into the very fabric of existence in every heartbeat, sunrise, and breath. Acknowledge his divine presence, and you shall find the strength to confront any challenge, for all things are possible with God.

CHAPTER 21

My Mind Is Sober

AS THE SIDE EFFECTS OF OBSTRUCTIVE SLEEP APNEA began to infiltrate my daily life, threatening to shroud me in a false acceptance of limitations, I recognised the subtle lie the devil sought to weave into my reality. In defiance, I clung to the powerful words of Philippians 2:5: *"Let this mind be in you, which was also in Christ Jesus."* It became my mantra, a declaration that my thoughts and beliefs would align with the divine strength God had placed within me.

Aware that the devil's conquest often begins with the mind, I stood firm when negative words assailed my identity and sought to derail my divine assignment. Drawing strength from Jeremiah 29:11, I anchored myself in the assurance that God's thoughts toward me were of peace, not of evil, with an expected end of triumph. My state of mind, I realised, was intricately linked to my success in life; to think as a failure was to become one, and conversely, to envision prosperity was to attract it.

Refusing to succumb to the negative narratives, I understood the power of words as seeds that take root and multiply. To counteract the effects of negative narratives, I deliberately fed my mind with the nourishment of positivity, favour, blessings, and prosperity found in the word of God. It became imperative to fortify my mind, creating a stronghold against the relentless assaults on my well-being.

In this battle for mental resilience, I embraced the truth of self-affirmation:

> *"I Am"*
> *I am who I believe myself to be and will never achieve it unless I declare it. With unwavering determination, I reclaim the self-ensuring truth and affirm my identity against the backdrop of adversity.*
> ***– Nikeisha Henlon-Sterling***

The chapter unfolds as a powerful testament to the transformative journey of renewing the mind, an essential battlefront against the attacks on the mind.

"The key to success is to focus our conscious mind on things we desire not things we fear." - Brian Tracy

My dear friends... If you want to get through life, you have to prepare to change your mindset. You must prepare to dump procrastination and unearth intentionality.

CHAPTER 22

I Will Walk With God Daily

IN MY DAILY LIFE'S CHAOTIC HUSTLE AND BUSTLE, the commitment to walk with God became a lofty goal amidst the relentless demands of work, home, studies, parenting, and wifely duties. The balance I aimed for was a complex juggle, a process where mistakes were unavoidable, and achieving harmony seemed like a challenging goal.

The early mornings, once dedicated to prayer and reflection, became battlegrounds for deadlines and responsibilities. The spiritual nourishment I often craved took a backseat to the pressing needs of the moment. As a parent, my heart ached with the constant tug-of-war between being present for my children and meeting the demands of my professional and academic pursuits. The role of a wife, too, seemed to bear the weight of expectations that threatened to overshadow the sacred bond we shared.

As I faced these challenges, I wrestled with guilt and a sense of inadequacy. The time once reserved for God became fragmented, swallowed by the demands of a life in a never-ending motion.

However, a triumphant story emerged within the chaos – a beacon of hope and inspiration. In the midst of the storm, I discovered that my perceived shortcomings did not limit God's grace. The challenges that threatened to derail my spiritual journey became opportunities for divine intervention.

Triumph was found in the small victories—stolen moments of prayer during a hectic day, finding solace in a verse during a moment of turmoil, and realising that God's presence was not confined to a specific time or place. The breakthrough came when I recognised that my daily walk with God was not about perfection but about the sincere intent of my heart.

Amidst the chaos, I found a reason to sing. The challenges, once seen as barriers, transformed into stepping stones, propelling me forward on my spiritual journey. I had to be intentional, as life's daily demands made no allotment for prayer and meditation. I prayed...

"Take my life and let it be,
Consecrated, Lord, to thee;
Take my hands, and let them move
At the impulse of Thy love,
At the impulse of Thy love.
Take my will, and make it Thine,
It shall be no longer mine;
Take my heart, it is Thine own!

It shall be Thy royal throne,
It shall be Thy royal throne." - Francis
Ridley Havergal

My dear friends... In the hustle and bustle of everyday life, where the pursuit of spiritual connection seems daunting amid work, family, and personal obligations, know that you're not alone. I've navigated the same challenges, wrestled with the same guilt and felt the weight of expectations. Yet, amidst the chaos, I discovered that God's grace extends beyond our perceived shortcomings. The key lies not in perfection but in the sincerity of your heart. Embrace the small victories, find solace in chaos, and remember that your divine walk is a continuous conversation with God, even in the busiest seasons.

CHAPTER 23

I Can Achieve Greatness

I AM NOT THE TYPE WHO GIVES UP QUICKLY. Failure, therefore, is never something that I contemplate, even when my mind tells me to give up. I have several long-term goals, and I am determined to achieve them. I firmly believe that:

> *"In order to successfully navigate your future, you must first overcome the challenges of the past."*
> ***– Nikeisha Henlon-Sterling***

Life is precious and deserving of our time and energy. Therefore, I cannot allow past failures to stifle what is possible. In my pursuit of greatness, I have changed how I approach every situation. I must adopt a winner's mindset and allow the title of an influential book to encapsulate my life.

"Change Your Thinking Change Your Life." - Brian Tracy

Expanding my horizons, reaching for the stars, and overcoming insurmountable obstacles is always possible. I have the potential to achieve greatness, to break free from the constraints that hold me back - I can, I must, and I will! I often remind myself that:

"It is great to be picked up by someone else, but it is even greater when you can pick your own self up."
– Nikeisha Henlon-Sterling

There are different measures of greatness, and each person defines greatness based on their thinking. I believe I achieve greatness when I overcome my debilitating circumstances and walk according to God's calling on my life. I will visualise the success I want to accomplish, just as I envision myself featured one day on the programme: "Profile" and becoming a school Principal.

My dear friends... Let your dreams be the fuel that drives you forward. Stay on course and ask God to help you to navigate your way.

CONCLUSION

AS THE FINAL PAGES OF THIS MEMOIR TURN, I am not bidding farewell to my story but embracing the infinite possibilities beyond these written words. I reflect not just on the trials endured and the triumphs celebrated but on the transformative journey that has shaped the very essence of who I am. Each challenge has been a crucible, refining my character and fortifying my resolve. As I stand on the precipice of the unknown, I carry with me the scars of battles fought, each mark telling a story of resilience, courage, and relentless determination. The pages of this memoir bear witness to the raw authenticity of my experiences — the moments of despair and the glorious victories that emerged from the depths of adversity.

With twists and turns, struggles, and triumphs, this journey is not a conclusion but a launchpad for what awaits. This is not just a concluding chapter but an anthem of empowerment. It's a proclamation that adversity, rather than a barrier, is a stepping stone to greatness. Every setback has been a setup for a comeback, and every tear shed has watered the seeds of growth. The storms I weathered were not meant to break me; they were catalysts for unveiling my true strength.

As the ink dries on these final pages, it marks not an end but a beginning – a beginning of a life postured towards boundless potential. The journey doesn't terminate with the last word; it takes flight into the realms of possibility. The struggles were not stumbling blocks but the path that led me to my triumphs.

The final message is gratitude for the hardships that sculpted my resilience, the triumphs that crowned my efforts, and the unwavering support of those who walked alongside me. As the last sentence fades, it carries the powerful refrain: the story continues, and the best is yet to come.

In this concluding chapter, I extend my final invitation:

My dear friends... Embark on your journey, face your challenges with unwavering courage, and celebrate your victories, no matter how small.

ACKNOWLEDGEMENT

To the Almighty Father who inspired me to write this book, I give thanks to you.

Thank you, Alfred Sterling, my dear husband, for leading me into pursuing this dream.

To my daughters, thank you for encouraging me to walk in my purpose; you have been my most loyal supporters.

Thank you to my friends and colleagues who have encouraged me on this journey and provided spiritual and moral support.

About the Author

Nikeisha Henlon-Sterling, an Edupreneur, Author, and Motivational Speaker, has been a member of the teaching fraternity for over 22 years. She is a Christian who believes God gave her a divine assignment.

The challenges brought on by Obstructive Sleep Apnea ultimately became the crucible for the forging of Nikeisha's indomitable spirit. It allowed her to be a survivor and a beacon of inspiration for those navigating the labyrinth of their trials.

Her spiritual experiences and the study of the Word of God laid the foundation for the unique perspective shared in her memoir. This story was inspired by God and affirmed by her mother.

Nikeisha is a passionate advocate for self-empowerment, channelling her energy into positively impacting the world. The experiences shared in her memoir are not just personal anecdotes but a testament to the resilience of the human spirit and the transformative power of one individual's journey.

She invites readers to glimpse into her life and glean valuable insights, finding resonance and strength in the shared human experience.

Nikeisha's story reminds us that every obstacle surmounted and every triumph celebrated contributes to the collective narrative of triumph over adversity.

www.ingramcontent.com/pod-product-compliance
Lightning Source LLC
LaVergne TN
LVHW010458160826
845677LV00012B/2538

* 9 7 8 9 7 6 6 5 5 1 3 4 6 *